PULSATION *of* LOVE

PULSATION *of* LOVE

GURUMAYI CHIDVILASANANDA

A SIDDHA YOGA® PUBLICATION / PUBLISHED BY SYDA FOUNDATION

www.siddhayoga.org

Gurumayi Chidvilasananda and Swami Muktananda
1982   Gurudev Siddha Peeth, Ganeshpuri, India

PULSATION *of* LOVE

Published by SYDA Foundation
PO Box 600, 371 Brickman Rd, South Fallsburg, NY 12779-0600, USA

COVER PHOTOGRAPH

The doors to Swami Muktananda's Samadhi Shrine in Gurudev Siddha Peeth, India,
stand partly open, offering a glimpse into the heart of the beautiful, austere memorial—
his final resting place. Pilgrims from all over the world journey to this radiant sanctuary,
seeking and receiving the unending grace of Gurumayi's Guru, the great Siddha master
whose love pulsates in every verse of this collection. Photo by Gerhard Ortner.

EDITOR'S NOTE

The poems in *Pulsation of Love* were originally published in limited edition
under the title *Ashes at My Guru's Feet*. This newly revised edition includes
all the poems from the original volume.

Once again we offer grateful appreciation to the poet George Franklin
for his vibrant support in preparing the poems for publication. We extend
thanks also to Valerie Sensabaugh, the managing editor; Cheryl Crawford,
the designer; and Patricia Stratton-Orloske and Barbara Yaffe, who super-
vised production.

Everyone connected with the publication of these verses has offered
service with genuine kindness of heart and loving dedication. Thank you
so much, each one, for your valuable contribution.

Kshama Ferrar, editor

Printed in the United States of America

First published 1990 under the title *Ashes at My Guru's Feet*. Second edition 2001

10 09 08 07 06 05 04 03 02 01   5 4 3 2 1

Library of Congress Cataloging-in-Publication Data is on page 77.

CONTENTS

FOREWORD

𝒪NE DAY MANY YEARS AGO, I was crossing a border between two countries in the Middle East. I had been sent there by the BBC to report on the art and culture of these countries, so I had with me some recording equipment and tapes—essential tools of my trade as a radio broadcaster and journalist. But that was not how I was seen by the border guards. What they thought was—Espionage! Government agent! Spy!

After some interrogation, they took me to a room, sat me on a chair, and told me they had dismissed my car and driver. They left me there alone with my imagination and fears. Night began to fall. Two young men in suits came and told me to follow them. They led me to a car. We drove into the dark without switching on the headlights. There were no street lights. As I recall, there was no light at all, not outside nor inside my own mind either. After ten minutes of driving, the car stopped. We were in the middle of nowhere, surrounded by desert. The young men both stepped out of the car. They said nothing; they had said nothing for the entire trip. They disappeared into the dark for what felt to me like hours.

I was truly terrified. After a while, I summoned the courage to peer out of the window and looked up into the night sky. It was a moonless night: the sky was studded with a canopy of stars, brilliant dots of pure light. As I looked, I heard the words rise from inside me: "As above, so below."

I knew intuitively what these words meant. I could feel an expansion inside me as vast as the sky. Anxiety dissolved. I felt peace, acceptance — for only God's will would take place, and I was safe in His hands. Love was throbbing in my heart, and I became aware of a genuine longing to know God. The two men returned to the car and drove me on to my original destination, a hotel some fifty miles away. They left me there with apologies, and I completed my assignment in safety and freedom.

That experience of the vast sky surges up in my memory again and again as I read this volume of verse by Gurumayi Chidvilasananda. Her vision of the journey to enlightenment is as vast and awesome as that night sky inlaid with the light of countless heavenly bodies. And yet for all this immensity, the striking imagery of her verse flows with a unique simplicity. In this, her first book of poems, Gurumayi speaks of the holy stages one traverses on the way to mastery of the spiritual path.

> The most exquisite of all breakthroughs
> is to pass beyond the death zone

of your ignorance,
to be smashed by the wave of grace
which enfolds you in its womb
and offers you as a sacrifice
to the mantle of God.

Then life knows what you are,
and you know what life is.

The poems in this volume, originally published in limited edition under the title *Ashes at My Guru's Feet,* describe the fulfillment of Gurumayi's quest not only for spiritual knowledge but also for the fullness of divine love. As Gurumayi writes about initiation, the Guru, and grace, she offers us an intimate glimpse into the Master's compassion for the seeker of Truth. "When you are following the spiritual path, the Guru's compassion strengthens your interest. His compassion is revealed in every posture of your life."

Gurumayi is the head of the Siddha Yoga lineage of spiritual Masters. As is true of saints in all traditions, the Siddhas of her lineage embody the conscious, divine energy that is the very fabric of creation. In the tradition of her lineage, the power to awaken seekers to this same divine force within themselves is passed from Master to chosen disciple. The poems in *Pulsation of Love* are an extraordinary testament to the inner transformation, initiated and guided by Gurumayi's own Master, Swami Muktananda, that led her to accepting from him the mantle of Guruhood.

To come into contact with a perfected Master is like entering the laboratory of an alchemist. "The Guru ... molds you into pearls of wisdom, pearls of dignity, pearls of surrender, pearls of tenderness and beauty." This process begins with a physical meeting, by reading or hearing the Master's words, or through the power of the Master's will. However it occurs, this yogic initiation, known as shaktipat, is a pivotal event in a seeker's life. With compassionate grace, the Siddha Guru awakens the aspirant's divine inner energy. After this awakening, the possibility of spiritual fulfillment immediately opens before us.

The night before my first visit to Shree Muktananda Ashram, the Siddha Yoga retreat center in upstate New York, I dreamed that Gurumayi brushed my head with a sheaf of peacock feathers. As the feathers touched me, I could feel an electric current send shivers down my back, and I called out, "This is shaktipat!" In the dream, Gurumayi beckoned me to come nearer until I stood close enough for her to touch me with her hand. Then, tapping above my heart with the tips of her fingers, she said again and again, "It is *there!*" A nurturing warmth spread through my being.

Two days later, I was walking on one of the garden paths of the ashram. To my utter delight, Gurumayi passed close by. She stopped right in front of me and began to ask me questions about myself: "Where do you live?" "What work do you do?" As Gurumayi was speaking with me, she began to tap with her fingertips on the very place above my heart that she had touched in my dream. Amidst the lightheartedness, her touch was awakening in me an ancient memory, a homecoming for which I had been longing. There again was that feeling of warmth I had experienced in my dream.

As time passed, I came to know that this feeling of homecoming is not, in fact, the journey's end, but rather the beginning of the path to true self-fulfillment. In order to move forward from what seems to be the darkness of sleep into the resplendent light of true awakening, we must become extremely strong in resolve, pure in intention, and more and more capable of receiving blessings. Gurumayi writes:

> To experience God's unending blessings,
>   your head must be clear.
> To know the compassion that ceaselessly flows,
>   your being must become like a river of milk.

As the disciple grows in spiritual practice and wisdom, so, too, does the intensity of his or her connection and love for God and the Guru. The inner being of the disciple becomes like a temple in which the pulsation of love is enthroned.

> Baba, your sweet fire sings its song
>   in the space of my heart.
> Your sweet fire dances its dance
>   in the palace of my heart.
> Your sweet fire of love conceals itself
>   in the cave of my heart.

This book is a love story, a tale of heroism, sacrifice, and an unbending will to attain unity with the divine Beloved. To enter the gate of the Beloved's heart, the duality of lover and Beloved must be erased, as must finally all of the seeker's doubts. Gurumayi recollects some questions that arose in her own mind just before she was escorted to the Vedic ceremony in which she was installed as successor in the lineage of Siddhas. But then, as though addressing her own thoughts, she says:

> Why question anymore
>> when "I" no longer remained
>> to hear the answer?

In these pages, we watch as Gurumayi transcends the passing pageantry of ordinary human reality. Though the wheel of her existence continues to turn, she has become, through her Guru's grace, unshakably united with its very center. Describing her arrival at the journey's end, the cradle of pulsating love, she says:

> When I lifted my head from Baba's feet,
>> I saw through two blurry eyes
>> that they were wet with my tears.
> My whole being was the charred
>> remains of his love. . . .
>
> I heard him say, "You are me."
> I said, "I am you."
> And everything fell
>> into the vast silence of love.

This is not a mere intellectual feat. This is the harvest of total and boundless surrender to the will of God and to one's spiritual path. This is indeed the adoration that Sufis call *fana'*, in which complete identification with the Beloved leaves no trace of the lover behind. Gurumayi says:

> As your sweet, enchanting form
>   became my goal,
>   an incredible thing happened—
>   I disappeared. . . .
>
>   nothing was left to describe;
>   the sole reality
>   was the experience of God.

Gurumayi's love courses throughout these poems in untamed imagery. Love is the whirling ecstasy of the "raging fire within," of that "wild and mad" love from which there is no escape, a love that takes all and gives everything. In the fire of love for the Master, the dross that holds our hearts back from God is burnt and "whatever remains is His work of art."

Gurumayi's words in these poems touch all aspects of my life. Sometimes as I pass through difficult stations of my own journey, I find myself repeating her utterances as though they were my own.

> It thundered; it poured.
> The lightning bolts smiled.
> Was I shattered to pieces?
> Or was I in the process of becoming whole?

Since I earn my livelihood with words, as a radio commentator, the wisdom she puts forward here has had a particularly profound effect on my work. I have learned, for instance, a new respect for the creative power of words. I have learned to look at world events with care and yet to view them, together with all the changing phases of my own life, as passing reflections seen in the mirror of my mind's eye.

Most significantly, I have received from this book the conviction that Gurumayi's words rise up from the mystic sea of God's love. Out of that love, she speaks to me and to you and to everyone who reads these words:

> "I could never tell you before,
> but now I want you to know
> you have come here because
> I wanted it to be so."

GEORGE MASRI
LONDON ▪ JUNE 2000

GEORGE MASRI grew up in the village of Madaba in Jordan. At an early age, he moved to England, where he trained as an actor and director. Later, he joined the BBC World Service as a presenter and producer in drama, documentaries, and current affairs. In 1975, he was initiated into the order of Mevlana Rumi's Whirling Dervishes. A decade later, he met Gurumayi in London, and since that time he has embraced the practices and teachings of the path of Siddha Yoga.

PULSATION *of* LOVE

THE FIRE OF MY LOVE

The fire of my love blazes
    through the crystal of my heart.
Just picture the colorful patterns
    of the fiery flames.
Just imagine the heat
    of the fire's brilliant blaze.

When that fire of love is reflected
    through the crystal of my heart,
    you can imagine what its glory must be
    and how divine a sight it is.

You know my love exists for you;
    and when you touch it,
    its patterns sweep
    through my entire being.

Every pore of my body is
    a spark of love for you.

I AM NOT THE SAME

I was warned about the flames of love.
This love is merciless;
    it ravages your heart.
From its heat you become wild and mad.
So mysterious is its energy
    that when it seizes you,
    you become impassioned
    and run about frenzied.
People sense in you the sparks of love,
    but they cannot see
    the raging fire within.

This love is tantalizing.
It wholly possesses you;
    it does not fill your heart and mind alone.
How it courses through every cell of your being!
It is brighter than lightning;
    it is more deafening than thunder;
    it pours over you
    more intensely than a cloudburst.

You can fantasize endlessly about love.
But remember: you can never bend it to your will.
It is independent, very free, very free.

Having known all its intricacies and madness,
    I still dived into the flames of love.
I cannot say what has happened to me, except
        I am not the same,
        I am not the same,
        I am not the same.

Baba, I give thanks to God
    for having your form
    incarnate on this earth.
Through your form,
    I have come to love
    the most elusive nature of God.

As I began my search,
    your form was my inspiration.
Whenever I lost trust,
    your form was still ablaze
    with the light of God.
And so I would begin again,
    and would continue my search
    with greater faith.

As your sweet, enchanting form
    became my goal,
    an incredible thing happened—
    I disappeared.
As I went still deeper into you,
    form itself dissolved;
    nothing remained but light—
    boundless, radiant light!

No color, no sound, no touch,
    no smell, no taste survived.
Beyond the grasp of the senses,
    nothing was left to describe;
    the sole reality
    was the experience of God.
Once again, an incredible thing happened—
    as I came to, the light of God
    condensed into your form.

O my Baba, you are God incarnate
    in a human form—
    no wonder, no wonder
    that I love you!

THOU ART THAT

My Guru is the fire of love.
His look, his word, his touch, his will
    shoot lightning throughout my being.

When I feel that his look has erased me,
    I am struck by his word,
    and I realize that there is still further to go;
When I believe that there is nothing more,
    I am blessed with his touch;
When I think that there is no more of me,
    the fire of his will immolates me.

At times his love is too great to bear.
The breath goes wild within me.
Thoughts become scattered,
    and the moods that underlie action
    have no aim, no destination.

I wonder: "What will all this accomplish?
    Is there any hope?
    Is there any meaning?
    Is there any purpose?"

I watch the blazing fire of his love
    consume every particle
    within and without,
    and am left with nothing.

Then once again his look, his word,
    his touch, and his will
    mold me into the form of his love.
It is evident that the fire of that love
    is both the destroyer and the creator.

The Guru reduces you to ashes through his love,
    then molds you into pearls of wisdom,
    pearls of dignity, pearls of surrender,
    pearls of tenderness and beauty.

Finally, he absorbs all the pearls into one
    called the Blue Pearl.

Then he gives you back to yourself,
    saying, "Thou art That."

MY BEING HAS BECOME YOU

What a beautiful moment it was
    when you looked into my eyes.
There was something in that look—
What was it? Were you aware of it?
It was powerful, yet very tender,
    beyond the grasp of this world.
Later you told me it was love.
You took me by surprise.
Still, I understood it was my destiny.

Yes, your love is my destiny.
Having known only its surface,
    now I yearn to plumb its depths.
Perhaps it is unfathomable.
Every pore of the body, mind, and heart
    must be saturated with it.

I stay here; but no, no, I live with you,
    and you fill me with your love.
Do you know it is your love
    that pours out of me?
My being has become you.
Baba, you are my love.
My heart throbs
    with the pulsation of your love.

LOVE'S SWEET FIRE

Through the fire of love, O my Baba,
  you keep me pure and close to you.
I never believed that I would be here
  and you would be there.
Destiny has played an inscrutable game.
But O my Baba,
  through the fire of love
  you sustain me
  in your own effulgent being.
Your love gives force to my breathing,
  to my speaking, to my very life.
It is your love that holds me together
  in this disintegrating world
  and in the world of Truth.

The Upanishads glorify your love.
The scriptures point to your love.
But the fire of your love is self-evident.
It is its own teaching, its own song.

O my Baba, you are so merciful!
All else will vanish,
    but your love will remain.
Your love is nectar;
    your love is life;
    your love is immortality.

The fire of your love
    creates form and dissolves it,
    gives rise to thought and dissolves it,
    brings about action and dissolves it.

Discrimination and detachment
    are the two tongues
    of the fire of your love.
As this fire blazes eternally in my heart,
    I watch countless sparks leap out of it
    and fall back into it.
When this is the case,
    what is action, and what is inaction?

Baba, your sweet fire sings its song
in the space of my heart.
Your sweet fire dances its dance
in the palace of my heart.
Your sweet fire of love conceals itself
in the cave of my heart.

May your grace always protect
this fire of love;
may your grace always nurture it.
O Baba, never separate me
from your sweet fire.

No more existence!
No more separation!
All that is, is nothing
but the blazing flame of your love.

You are my love.
Love is you.
What else is there but love?

MY PRAYER TO BABA

O Baba, let me live forever in the universe
     in which you dwell.
Never leave me,
     and never allow me to leave you.
With your grace, Baba,
     may I always breathe
     the air that you breathe.
With your grace
     may I always see what you see.
With your grace, Baba,
     may I walk the same path
     that you walk.
May I be lost in the love of my Guru,
     just as you are lost
     in the love of yours.
O Baba, to live in a universe
     other than yours
     would be worse than living in hell.

I know that my Guru has heard my prayer.
He has given me everything I wish for.
He has miraculously transformed himself
     into the subtlest, most divine love
     that can ever exist in this universe.

Drinking this love, sometimes I drown,
    sometimes I soar.
Yet there is no touching bottom
    nor reaching the top.
O Baba, all that exists is your love,
    the love of my Guru, the love that is you.

God is so kind, yet people tend
    to forget His generosity.
For this reason He has created
    some grateful people
    to remind the forgetful ones
    that His abundant blessings
    are the source of everyone's life.

Thanking God is indispensable.
When you give thanks to God
    enormous joy
    flows through your life.
The happier you grow inside
    the brighter your world becomes.
Finally, you feel God's love everywhere.

I thank God for my Guru, Muktananda.
And I thank my Guru for the God
    he has revealed within me.

But I hear my Guru laughing—
      why does he laugh?
Perhaps he wants to see
      how I will thank him.
Yes, he is right. He is me, I am him;
      when this is the case
      who is going to thank whom?

And yet there is such great grace
      in loving and thanking my Guru
      that I want to be separate from him
      though always remembering we are one.

O Baba, you are the *rasa* of my life.
Your love is the light of my life.
O Baba, you are love itself.

Thank you, thank you, thank you.

THE MASTER OF LIFE'S PLAY

How often you sent for me!
Yet the reasons were always hidden from me.
Every time I came
    I had a strong feeling
    that the reason you had called me
    was yet to be revealed to me.

I looked at you,
    but you ignored my gaze.
When I asked you mentally,
    you gave me a blank look.

When I became uncomfortable,
    you made things easy;
    but when I felt better,
    you started yelling at me.

I never knew what to do before you.
If I put my feet in the water,
    you didn't like it;
    if I put them in the fire,
    you were puzzled by my ignorant ways.

O Baba! This no, that no,
    this yes, that yes.
What is really no,
    and what is really yes?
What is a smile, and what is a frown?

You are amazing!
You encompass everything!
You enact a drama,
    and you also watch it.

O Baba! You love it. I know you do!
The Self is the actor,
    the Self is the stage,
    and the senses are the spectators.

My Baba is the master of this play.

LIFE OF MY LIFE

You have understood me
        just as I understand myself;
Yet you have known me
        as I have never known myself.
You are great. I understand this
        as you work through me;
Yet you are greater than great,
        for you escape the reaches
        of my understanding.
You are my feelings,
        but you are not limited.
You are my thoughts,
        but you are not transitory.
You are my actions,
        but you are not bound.
You want me to know you
        in the way I must know you.
You change nothing, though changes
        keep taking place.
You are so detached,
        and yet, O life of my life,
I cannot stop loving you.

GURU PURNIMA

Guru Purnima,
    the celebration of all celebrations,
    is the day devoted
    exclusively to the Guru.
All days and nights
    are nothing but the pulsation
    of the Guru's Shakti.
And yet, O my beloved Guru Muktananda,
    Guru Purnima is that day and night
    when even the moon
    reveals its full luster,
    when all days and nights
    have reached their culmination
    and are in suspension, awaiting
    a glimpse of their own Master.

O Guru Muktananda,
    though you are the embodiment
    of all that divine energy,
Though you carried the message
    of your own Gurudev,
    Bhagawan Nityananda,

Though you imparted all the teachings
        to everyone who came before you,
        who thought of you, saw your picture,
        read your books, or dreamt of you,
Never for a moment
        did you stop showing your gratitude
        to your own beloved Guru.
All that you did
        you attributed to the grace
        of Bhagawan Nityananda.
You considered yourself a blade of grass
        in the court of your Guru.
Such humility, such divine love, such surrender!
No wonder you became everything
        that thousands of people
        experienced within themselves.

Today is the most auspicious day.
It is so divinely auspicious
        because of your existence.
You are the Guru
        who transforms even nothing
        into everything good.

Your presence makes this day
     even more special.
Your existence makes every day worth living.
Your knowledge and your wisdom
     make life resplendent.

You loved this day above all others
     when you lived on earth in a physical body,
     because you could show
     more gratitude to your Guru.
Your whole being was the worship
     of Bhagawan Nityananda.
You sang for him, you talked for him,
     you cooked for him, you dressed for him.

You have made the Guru's Shakti come alive.
Although the Guru's Shakti
     is constantly pulsating,
     somehow you infuse it
     with even more *prana*.

On the day of Guru Purnima,
    you looked like Lord Shiva.
You revealed something unique and secret
    to those who had the eyes to perceive.
You imparted the Guru's Shakti
    even more obviously than at other times.
You brought out more devotion to the Guru,
    even in the driest of hearts.

What a name you have!
The sweetest name—Muktananda.
I can live just singing your name,
    Muktananda, Muktananda,
    O my beloved Muktananda!

I want to garland you,
    but where can I find the flowers
    that are not already yours?

I want to wrap you in a warm shawl,
    but what can be warmer
    than your own being?

I want to adorn you
    with the most beautiful sandals,
    but how can I make any sandals
    fit *So'ham*, which are your feet?

I want to wave the lights for you,
    but will I see that flame
    before your effulgence?

You are so great and so divine,
    how can I do anything for you?
You are everything I see, hear, taste, and touch.
You are everywhere I go.
You are universal Being,
    that vibrating, scintillating, dynamic Shakti.

If you ever wish to become very small,
    then let me know
    so I can play with you.
Otherwise, on this day of Guru Purnima,
    I can only offer
    my salutations to you
    in all directions.

May the wind carry my message to you,
    may the fire illumine it,
    may the water keep it moist,
    may the earth keep it solid,
    and the ether keep it pure.

O my sweet Muktananda!
Seated within, it is you
    who make me say all this.
    What must I do? —

You are the inspiration of my life,
    which has been offered
    at your feet.

Jaya Guru Muktananda!
Jaya Guru Muktananda!
Jaya Guru Muktananda!

INITIATION

Initiation occurs once in a lifetime.
Actions carry with them feelings and emotions.
The merits of many lifetimes, together with grace,
    bring about the divine action known as *diksha*.

The experience of initiation
    is worth every drop of life's blood.
The moment a seeker is initiated, he becomes That.
He finds a shady tree to cool himself
    from the heat of worldly bondage.

When I met my Guru,
    I was struck by the lightning of love.
I thought that was it, and I lived in it.
A few years later, I was struck again by that lightning.
It was then revealed to me as Shaktipat.
Once again I thought that I had come
    to the end of the cycle,
        and I began to adapt my life to it.

That life lasted for many, many years in this world,
    though it went by in a flash.
Every second with my Guru contained a million years.

When he gave me Shaktipat,
 he began his conscious work on me.
He revealed the Truth to me in many ways.

Of course, I was not always aware
 of what was being thrown in my path.
Sometimes it was love, sometimes it was envy,
 sometimes it was harsh words,
 sometimes sweetness, sometimes utter bliss,
 sometimes the feeling of eternal life,
 and sometimes a sense
 of life's fleeting nature.

I did not let any one of these pass by
 without examining it:
I looked at it, felt it, and took care of it.

The grace of Shaktipat
 was omniscient and penetrating;
 whatever was meant to stay with me remained
 and the rest was offered to the fire of yoga.
Through grace alone I was able to live
 and watch as each fold of life was unfurled,
 and then removed from my sight.
Finally, everything dissolved into one thing: love.

Time unceasingly did its work,
    making everything except love
    vanish from before my eyes.

The subject of my taking *sannyasa*
    was brought up when I was off guard.
This was something I wanted, but it was never clear
    what it would mean in my life.

I had questions: "Do I really need it?
Is it just a way to escape the world?
Is it ego or is it a gift? Why do I need it?
Don't I already have enough labels
    with which to identify myself?
Do I want yet another one to store
    in the bank of my memory?"

But there was a greater power within me,
    more potent than the questions and doubts.
It wanted to explode and stampede over me.
It was frightening, yet soothing at the same time.

My Gurudev let me wallow
in my questions, in my doubts.
At times he supported me;
at times he disapproved
of what I was thinking.

My feelings covered such a wide range:
sometimes divine, sometimes ridiculous.
At times I was the idol in a temple,
and at times a mere blade of grass.
Like a shy plant, I sometimes felt open,
but when the breeze of power blew
in my direction, I would close.

My Guru was compassionate
and willing to bear with me.
It was his love, it was his heart,
that allowed me to live through everything.

At last the day arrived: April 26, 1982.
My Guru sheared off my hair;
he clothed me in a white sari
and shot the dragon's fire at me.
Maha Shaktipat took place.

For days on end I walked in that light,
 slept in that light, ate in that light.
Everything within and without
 was bathed in white light.
No more questions, no more doubts,
 no more of those things
 that had gnawed at me.

I was gone.
I don't know how I left;
 I only know that grace took me away
 and began to install *purno'ham.*

The final day arrived: May 8, 1982.
Not much remained to be killed.
There was only the physical body
 that had to be covered,
 not in a white sari
 but in orange cloth—
 the color of the fire
 which had been shot at me.

That morning I went to my Guru's room
    and did a full *pranam*.
I looked at him; he looked at me.
How many times can one melt
    when one has already melted completely?
So much love, so much Shakti!
Did my poor body have enough strength
    to contain all this?

I was told that everything
    would take place in the Yajna Mandap
    at the most auspicious of auspicious times:
    my Guru's birthday.

But was he ever really born
    or did he always exist?
Was all this just a game?

Why question anymore
    when "I" no longer remained
    to hear the answer?

I took my seat in the Yajna Mandap
near the blazing fire.
My Guru was seated on his throne,
but in that place deep within me,
near the fire, he exploded
And became everything in the universe for me.

It thundered; it poured.
The lightning bolts smiled.
Was I shattered to pieces?
Or was I in the process of becoming whole?

Initiation occurs once in a lifetime,
although experiences are many
and come at different times.

This was when *purno'ham* was installed
in place of Swami Chidvilasananda.
The perfect "I"-consciousness,
purno'ham vimarsha,
is the gift of the Siddhas.
My Guru, out of his compassion,
turned base metal into gold.
Whatever remains is his work of art.
Everything happens through his grace.

His grace flows through the mantra,
    which becomes a living companion to seekers.

The *paripurna diksha,*
    more complete than the complete,
    took place on this day.

There is nothing left to do
    except to sit humbly
    at the feet of my Guru;
There is nothing more to say.

BREAKTHROUGH

Life is so many things for so many people.
For one person, it is to become a householder;
    for another, an ascetic.
For one, to earn more and more money;
    for another, to live a life of poverty.
For one, to rejoice in violence;
    for another, complete indifference.
For one, to become famous;
    for another, to hide from the world.
For one, to become known by predicting the future;
    for another, by remaining silent.
Everyone has a different life.
And everyone has made sacrifices
    in so many ways.

What is the meaning behind this life?
Who is supposed to know whom?
Is life supposed to know you,
    or are you supposed to know life?

I know one thing about my life:
    the power of grace has taken me across.
While living,
    I have experienced the realm of death.

Offering one's life to the Master
   is the most benevolent
   and frightening experience.

My Guru gave me the knowledge
   of who is supposed to know whom—
   you or life.
Through the years that I was graced
   to spend with my Guru,
I experienced one breakthrough after another.

It was definitely his grace that gave me life.
But resistance, lack of understanding,
   and the inability to surrender
   created one wave after another.
I was struck by each wave and washed clean.

Each successive breakthrough
   came at the peak of intense *tapasya,*
   and it was also the fruit of that austerity.
Whether it came during waking, dreaming, or deep sleep,
   from the mantra, meditation, or seva,
   from a glance, a look, or a word from my Guru—
   he used everything to mold my life.

He was both tender and harsh,
    loving and rejecting, smiling and stern,
    all-embracing and transcendent.

Everything that happened
    begot the self-denial
    that led to the knowledge of the Self.

The tests came in many forms;
    sometimes they struck like lightning,
    and sometimes they were as smooth as flowing water.
Sometimes they were as sharp as a million needles,
    and sometimes they came cloaked
    in absolute numbness.

What was needed at all times was
    full faith and surrender.
If the doorframe is low,
    then bend your head and walk through it.
If the sword is brandished before you,
    lower your head, otherwise misfortune will result.

So it is in sadhana.
Make the life you choose to live a worthy one.
It is a matter of great fortune
    to rejoice in life
    having once sacrificed it.

Life is not like an abandoned fruit,
    yet it requires absolute sacrifice.

A life without grace bears no fruit.
Millions of lives can be lived,
    but for what purpose
    if there is no breakthrough?
The most exquisite of all breakthroughs
    is to pass beyond the death zone of your ignorance,
    to be smashed by the wave of grace
    which enfolds you in its womb
    and offers you as a sacrifice
    to the mantle of God.

Then life knows what you are,
    and you know what life is.

ASHES AT MY GURU'S FEET

One day Baba called me
    and spoke to me sweetly.
He asked me, "Are you ready to become ashes
    at the Guru's feet?"
I didn't know.
I panicked and couldn't look at him.
I kept my eyes on his beautiful feet.
In my mind, I knew they were my home;
    they were where I had always belonged.

Yet the question puzzled me.
With all my pride, my shortcomings, my limitations,
    how would I ever become
    ashes at my Guru's feet?
I *pranamed* and took my leave of him.

The next morning after the *Guru Gita*,
    a song was played throughout the ashram,
    "Become Ashes at the Guru's Feet."

I froze. Was it a message?
Was it a teaching? Was it a command?
I inquired of myself, I tortured myself,
    I looked very deeply within myself,
    but there was no answer.

The question remained unresolved,
    and my dilemma continued to grow.

The following morning I was sitting in the courtyard
    watching my beautiful Guru.
He was gentle to all who approached him.
He smiled and talked.
He observed and remained silent.

But I was not quiet.
I wondered if I was supposed to answer him,
    or if I was supposed to change.
My restlessness became unbearable.

Another day arrived.
The same inquisition took place within me.

Wandering through the ashram,
    I saw a picture of Baba bowing to his Guru.
As I watched the picture, it dissolved.
In its place I saw a beautiful flame.
Baba and his Guru were within it. I wept.

To become ashes at the Guru's feet
     is to merge into the Guru.
But how could that happen?

Again Baba called me.
He looked at me lovingly and asked,
     "Have you heard the song
     'Become Ashes at the Guru's Feet'?
     Isn't it the sweetest song
     you have ever heard?"

Again I was consumed by a powerful agony.
I wished I could disappear.
I wished I weren't such a rock.

All of a sudden, my Guru, my Baba,
     placed his hand on my head.
Streaks of fire exploded from his palm.
The house of my individuality was set ablaze.
Everything I had was burned away.

I wanted to save my house.
When that was impossible,
    I wanted to save a few possessions.
But I could not escape—
    the door of the house was also on fire.
I do not know what happened after that.

When I lifted my head from Baba's feet,
    I saw through two blurry eyes
    that they were wet with my tears.
My whole being was the charred
    remains of his love.

He began to sing,
    "Become ashes at the Guru's feet."
For the first time, a smile lit up my being.
He continued to sing.

The lightning of laughter flashed between us.
We looked at each other, simultaneously
    closing our eyes in supreme agreement.
I heard him say, "You are me."
I said, "I am you."
And everything fell
    into the vast silence of love.

A THOUSAND MIRRORS

A thousand mirrors were neatly placed
    on the table of my life.
Since life itself was an enigma,
    I looked for meaning in the reflections.

Each mirror had its own width and depth
    and also its own distortions.
Some reflections were smaller, and others larger;
    still others were totally out of proportion,
    yet they seemed to speak about life
    and shed meaning on existence.
I watched the myriad reflections
    of feelings, thoughts, and actions.

In the beginning it was all fun,
    like a child's game—
But the game was not distant from reality.

A thousand mirrors became my dwelling.
Time passed, watching.
It seemed a comfortable way of living.

Then the Guru's grace struck my life.
One by one, each mirror was shattered to pieces.
The reality of my existence was at stake.
The table of my life was shaking.

As grace continued to strike,
        each mirror was broken
        into thousands of fragments;
        the reflections became innumerable.
But now they no longer made sense.
Each single, clear reflection
        had become multifaceted.
One reflection of sadness became many.
One reflection of joy was also multiplied.
Yet nothing held true meaning anymore.

The Guru's grace continued to strike.
Ultimately, the last mirror, so dear to the heart,
        the mirror that maintained the difference
        between the individual soul
        and the Supreme Soul,
        was about to be destroyed.

My whole being wept.
My senses abandoned me.
My world crumbled.

Destruction took its time.
While grace was penetrating deeply,
    I said to myself,
    "People say grace is a shelter.
    Why, then, am I losing all I have?"

The last mirror,
    which gave me hope,
    which gave me support,
    which held my entire universe together,
    my dearest friend for lifetime after lifetime,
    was about to become the prey of grace.

The sword of light shone brilliantly.
Reflections melted in this mirror.
Finally, when the strongest mirror exploded,
    not even a trace remained
    of that existence which had once
    found meaning in reflections.

A wondrous thing had happened:
    all the reflections had become grace;
    all the mirrors had become grace.
Grace had revealed that everything is grace.

The Guru smiled as my nonexistent life
    merged into one truth—
    the love of my Guru.

The table of my life had vanished;
    my life itself
    had become the life of my Guru.

AS THE LIGHT
COMES STREAMING DOWN

As the light comes streaming down,
    yesterday, today, and forever,
    the air is draped with a white robe.
The rivers seem to flow with milk.
The entire earth rejoices
    with the tenderness of love.
The heart, too, expresses its thanks,
    being filled with the Lord's compassion,
    with His infinite blessings.

All times are God's time,
    and God's time is eternity.
Every soul knows this in its own depths,
    but does not always remember what it knows.
Thankfulness is the very nature of the soul.

By not remembering
    that all times are God's time
    you are only thankful
    for what seems to be good.
When you are born, it is time to thank God.
As life continues, it is time to thank God.
When you die, too, it is time to thank God.
Always this light is a blessing.
This light is compassion itself.

Today we have gathered here to celebrate
	the day of Gurumayi's birth.
But how can you celebrate another's birthday
	without including yourself in the celebration?
How can you be thankful for another's life
	if you are not thankful for your own?
How can you be truly part of a celebration
	without sharing in its ecstasy?

How can you love someone else
	if you have not felt your own heart?
How can you look at another with love
	if you are not in that love already?

Everlasting light streams down
	touching earth and heaven simultaneously,
	sustaining life in all three worlds.

This very light is the brilliance in words.
It is the vitality in plants and flowers.
It is the power that heals wounded hearts.
This light is the life of all.

It is possible for a heart to be thankful
	only when it realizes its infinite luminosity.
Then, whether you are passing through a dark tunnel
	or one bathed in light,
Whether you are being scorched by the noonday sun
	or anointed by a cooling balm,
Whether you are eating bitter crumbs
	or the sweetest delicacies,
Whether you are sitting on jagged coral
	or the softest sand,
There is nothing that you cannot bear.

As the light of your heart falls on all,
	your good karma constantly returns you
	to the love of your own heart.

The love of my heart is my Guru.
The power of his grace brought me back to him.
His presence on earth is the delight of my heart.
Whatever our relationship was in other lifetimes,
	in this lifetime it was most certainly
	the Guru-disciple relationship.

I ask God to give me enough time
     to thank Him for this relationship.
In the Guru-disciple relationship
     my being has become vast as well as tiny,
     manifest as well as unmanifest,
     great as well as small.
The grace of my Guru has taught my heart
     to be thankful for what has been given to me
     and also for what has not been given to me.

In 1975 Baba asked me to translate for him.
I did not speak English—at least not well enough
     to make any sense. So I asked him,
     "Baba, if you knew
     I would be translating for you,
     why didn't you force me
     to learn English long ago?"

He replied, "If I had asked you
     to learn English before,
     you would not be so thankful to learn it now.
     You would have had so much time on your hands.
     But now you have to learn it right away.
     Every minute you will be thankful
     for learning to speak the language."

I understood my Guru wanted to teach me humility.
If I had already learned the language
    I would have had the pride of learning.
Instead I felt only thankfulness
    for every word I could offer my Guru.

Another time, when I was still in school,
    Baba told me he would celebrate
    my sixteenth birthday in the ashram.
He talked about it to everyone.
He told me about all the grand things he would prepare
    and the gifts he was going to shower on me.

The day before my birthday
    I was supposed to go to Ganeshpuri,
    but God decided to open the heavens
    and send torrents of rain.
There was flooding everywhere.
No form of transportation was moving.
All night my heart was in despair.

The next day was my birthday.
I could still have gone to Ganeshpuri,
        but the Lord was not done with His blessings.
The rain was still pouring.
My heart was so troubled, so grave.
It did not feel any joy
        from the light streaming down.

The next weekend I went to Ganeshpuri.
My birthday was not mentioned,
        and I received no belated gift.
As I *pranamed* to say goodbye Sunday evening,
        Baba looked at me and asked,
        "Did you remember me on your birthday?"

His question was an arrow
        that struck the fountainhead of tears.
I realized that Baba's true gift
        was the remembrance of my Guru,
        not some external object.
And I had received the gift of remembering him.

I continually pined for my Guru—
   for his love, his fierceness, his kindness,
   his discipline, his generosity, his self-control,
   his grace, and his compassion.
He was in every moment of my day.

As Baba asked me his question
   I was riveted to the floor.
Everything melted into one bowl
   overflowing with his eternal love.
The silence was so profound!
I could not even hear
   the beating of my own heart.

Then Baba said, "I remembered you, also."
In the deepest silence,
   those words full of love
   opened a new dimension in my heart.

What else can I say but, "Thank you, Lord."
It is possible to count the blessings
   that you understand, but how can you count
   the blessings you do not understand?

Blessings are countless. Without blessings
      you cannot even take a single step.
God's blessings are there
      not only when your desires are fulfilled
      but even when they are not.
A thankful heart is aware of this.

In the Guru-disciple relationship
      the Guru's compassion
      is the *sudarshana chakra,*
      destroying evil and protecting good.
When you are following the spiritual path,
      the Guru's compassion strengthens your interest.
His compassion is revealed
      in every posture of your life.

Only a thankful heart will recognize it
      and experience his compassion,
Not just when you think you need it,
      but at every moment of your life.
How can words convey the Guru's compassion?
It makes no distinctions, knows no bounds.

Recently, I dreamed of Bade Baba.
His huge, dark body lay on a simple mat.
I had the good fortune to massage his body.
His skin was so tender, so soft!
With great care and love I was rubbing his chest.
And I was as gentle as I could be.

I asked him why his joints were so stiff,
        why he was having so much pain.
He turned his eyes toward me,
        and with the softest look he said,
        "If I did not take the pain
        of those who love me,
        what would become of them?
        This is not pain. It is their love."

His words, so filled with love,
        engulfed my entire being
        with infinite compassion.
No words can possibly describe what I felt.
Bade Baba was compassion incarnate.

The essence of the Guru-disciple relationship
        is the Guru's compassion.
It is limitless and unfathomable.
So subtle yet infinitely powerful,
        it takes a disciple across
        the ocean of birth and death.

These priceless gems—
        blessings, compassion, and thankfulness—
        are given to us all without measure.
They are never taken from us.

To be worthy of experiencing profound thanks,
        you must have devoted eyes,
        vision that is pure enough to perceive
        the light that is constantly streaming down.

To experience God's unending blessings,
        your head must be clear.
To know the compassion that ceaselessly flows,
        your being must become like a river of milk.

THE FORM
THAT I CAN ALWAYS LOVE

In the back of the meditation hall,
    in the alcove, I sat very still
    as my ears heard all about the Goddess Kundalini
    and my eyes perceived Her different forms
    on the screen.

Suddenly a bolt of energy
    shot through my body so intensely
    that my entire being became motionless,
    transfixed by the picture of my beloved Guru
    behind the Guru's *gaddi*.

His eyes were piercing me, and his entire being
    was moving to embrace me. It was so real!

A tender voice within me melodiously said to him,
    "O Goddess Kundalini,
    I am so happy you took this form
    that I could love all my life."

And it kept repeating itself:
    "The form that I can always love,
    the form that I can always love,
    the form that I can always love . . .
    which in turn takes me to the formless."

It all began in love
    and remained in love.
Finally, love dissolves in love. O Baba!
When I told you I wanted to offer my life to you,
    you asked me how far I would like to go.

I said, "If you could just give me grace and devotion,
    I would never want to see the end of my surrender."

You beamed, stroked my head, and said,
    "I could never tell you before,
    but now I want you to know
    you have come here because
    I wanted it to be so."

When you said that, Baba,
    you did something to me.
It is yet to be understood.

You are the form of God that I love.
Your form has bestowed everything.
It is through your form that I have been able
    to complete the journey within myself.

Your form is grace.
Your form is love.
Your form is a blessing.
Your form is everything
    I would ever want in my life.

How shall I worship you?
What hymns, what verses, what songs, what dances,
    what flowers, and what fruits—
    what elements must I use to worship you?

You dissolved me into your love,
    so there is no more "I" and "mine."
What I have is all from you.
How can I return your own gift?

So, my beloved Baba,
    if you take away the physical body
    and make it merge into your form,
    which I love to this day,
    perhaps song will merge into song,
    perhaps flame will merge into flame,
    and love will become love.
And that is what you are, my Gurudev.

In the *Guru Gita* I recite every day:

I remember Shri Guru who is Parabrahman,
I speak of Shri Guru who is Parabrahman,
I bow to Shri Guru who is Parabrahman,
I worship Shri Guru who is Parabrahman.

THE POEMS

THE POEMS

GURU PURNIMA
South Fallsburg, New York ~ July 1985

INITIATION
Los Angeles, California ~ May 1985

BREAKTHROUGH
South Fallsburg, New York ~ August 1985

ASHES AT MY GURU'S FEET
Ganeshpuri, India ~ December 1986

A THOUSAND MIRRORS
Ganeshpuri, India ~ January 1987

AS THE LIGHT COMES STREAMING DOWN
South Fallsburg, New York ~ June 1988

THE FORM THAT I CAN ALWAYS LOVE
South Fallsburg, New York ~ August 1986

GUIDE TO SANSKRIT PRONUNCIATION

For the reader's convenience, Sanskrit and Hindi terms appear throughout the text in roman type with simple transliteration. *Śaktipāta*, for instance, is shaktipat; *sādhana* is sadhana, and so on. The standard international transliteration for each Sanskrit term is given in brackets for the glossary entries.

For readers not familiar with Sanskrit, the following is a guide for pronunciation.

Vowels and Diphthongs

Sanskrit vowels are categorized as either long or short. In English transliteration, the long vowels are marked with a bar above the letter and are pronounced twice as long as the short vowels. The letters *e* and *o* are always pronounced as long vowels.

Short:	Long:	
a as in cup	*ā* as in calm	*ai* as in aisle
i as in give	*e* as in save	*au* as in cow
u as in full	*ī* as in seen	*ū* as in school
	o as in know	

Consonants

The main differences between Sanskrit and English pronunciation of consonants are in the aspirated and retroflexive letters.

The aspirated letters have a definite *h* sound. The Sanskrit letter *kh* is pronounced as in inkhorn; the *th* as in boathouse; the *ph* as in loophole.

The retroflexes are pronounced with the tip of the tongue touching the hard palate; *ṭ*, for instance, is pronounced as in ant; *ḍ* as in end.

The sibilants are *ś*, *ṣ*, and *s*. The *ś* is pronounced as *sh* but with the tongue touching the soft palate; the *ṣ* as *sh* with the tongue touching the hard palate; the *s* as in history.

Other distinctive consonants are these:

c as in church	*ṃ* is a strong nasal
ñ as in canyon	*ḥ* is a strong aspiration
ṛ as in written	

For a detailed pronunciation guide, see
The Nectar of Chanting, published by SYDA Foundation.

GLOSSARY

ASHRAM [*āśrama*]
The dwelling place of a Guru or saint; a monastic retreat site where seekers engage in spiritual practices and study the sacred teachings of yoga.

BABA [*bābā*]
A term of affection and respect for a saint or holy man.

BADE BABA
(*lit.,* elder Baba) An affectionate name for Bhagawan Nityananda, Baba Muktananda's Guru.

BLUE PEARL
A brilliant blue light, the size of a tiny seed, that appears to the meditator whose *kundalinī* energy has been awakened; it is the subtle abode of the inner Self.

DIKSHA [*dīkṣā*]
Yogic initiation; the spiritual awakening of a disciple by the grace of the Master. *See also* SHAKTIPAT.

GADDI
The seat of the Guru, invested with the power and authority of the lineage.

GANESHPURI [*gaṇeśapurī*]
A village in the Tansa River Valley in Maharashtra, India. Bhagawan Nityananda settled in this region, where yogis have performed spiritual practices for thousands of years. The ashram founded by Swami Muktananda at his Guru's command is built on this sacred land.

GURU [*guru*]
A spiritual Master who has attained oneness with God and who is able both to initiate seekers and to guide them on the spiritual path to liberation. A Guru is also required to be learned in the scriptures and must belong to a lineage of Masters. *See also* SHAKTIPAT; SIDDHA.

GURUDEV [*gurudeva*]
(*lit.,* divine teacher) A respectful term of address, signifying the Guru as an embodiment of God.

GURU GITA [*gurugītā*]
(*lit.,* song of the Guru) A sacred text consisting of mantras that describe the nature of the Guru, the Guru-disciple relationship, and techniques of meditation on the Guru. In Siddha Yoga ashrams, the *Guru Gītā* is chanted every morning.

GURU PURNIMA [*gurupūrṇimā*]
(*lit.,* the full moon of the Guru) In India, the full moon of the month of Ashada (July-August) is honored as the most auspicious and important of the entire year. This moon's luminous brilliance and perfect form are seen as expressions of the Guru's gift of grace and the attainment of Self-realization.

GURU'S FEET, GURU'S SANDALS
The Guru's feet are mentioned in most Indian scriptures, where they are said to embody Shiva and Shakti, knowledge and action, the emission and reabsorption of creation. Vibrations of the inner Shakti flow out from the Guru's feet. They are a mystical source of grace and illumination, and a figurative term for the Guru's teachings. Many beautiful and ancient hymns are addressed to them and

GLOSSARY

to the Guru's sandals, which are also said to hold the divine energy of enlightenment.

JAYA [*jaya*]
An exclamation of praise, generally translated as "Hail!"

KARMA [*karma*]
(*lit.*, action) 1) Any action—physical, verbal, or mental. 2) Destiny, which is caused by past actions, mainly those of previous lives.

KUNDALINI [*kuṇḍalinī*]
(*lit.*, coiled one) The supreme power, the primordial energy (shakti) that lies coiled at the base of the spine. Through the descent of grace (shaktipat), this extremely subtle force, also described as the supreme Goddess, is awakened and begins to purify the entire being. As Kundalini travels upward through the central channel, She pierces the various chakras, finally reaching the *sahasrāra* at the crown of the head. There, the individual self merges into the supreme Self and attains the state of God-realization. *See also* SHAKTI.

MAHA [*mahā*]
Great; mighty; powerful.

MANTRA [*mantra*]
(lit., sacred invocation) The names of God; sacred words or divine sounds invested with the power to protect, purify, and transform the individual who repeats them. A mantra received from an enlightened Master is filled with the power of her attainment.

PARABRAHMAN [*parabrahman*]
The all-pervasive, supreme Principle of the universe, whose nature is described as absolute Existence, Consciousness, and Bliss.

PARIPURNA DIKSHA [*paripūrṇadikṣhā*]
The ultimate initiation in which the disciple receives Self-realization from the Master.

PRANA [*prāṇa*]
The vital life-sustaining force of both the body and the universe.

PRANAM [*praṇāma*]
To bow; to show one's respect.

PURNO 'HAM [*pūrṇo 'haṃ*]
Perfect "I"-consciousness; awareness of one's inner divinity.

PURNO'HAM VIMARSHA [*pūrṇo 'haṃvimarśa*]
(*lit.*, the full "I am" awareness) The experience of complete identity with supreme Consciousness, within and without.

RASA [*rasa*]
Nectar, sweetness.

SADHANA [*sādhana*]
Spiritual discipline and practices, the spiritual journey.

SANNYASA [*saṁnyāsa*]
The ceremony and vows of monkhood, in the religious traditions of India.

SELF
Divine Consciousness residing in the individual, described as the witness of the mind or the pure "I"-awareness.

GLOSSARY

SEVA [*sevā*]

(*lit.*, service) Selfless service; work offered to God, performed without attachment and with the attitude that one is not the doer. In Siddha Yoga ashrams, seva is a spiritual practice, and students seek to perform all of their tasks in the spirit of selfless offering.

SHAKTI [*śakti*]

The divine Mother, dynamic spiritual energy; the creative force of the universe. *See also* KUNDALINI.

SHAKTIPAT [*śaktipāta*]

(*lit.*, descent of grace) Yogic initiation in which the Siddha Guru transmits her fully awakened spiritual energy into the aspirant, thereby awakening the aspirant's dormant kundalini shakti. *See also* DIKSHA; GURU; KUNDALINI.

SHIVA, LORD [*śiva*]

One of the Hindu trinity of gods, representing God as the destroyer, often understood by yogis as the destroyer of barriers to one's identification with the supreme Self. In his personal form, Shiva is portrayed as a yogi wearing a tiger skin and holding a trident.

SIDDHA [*siddha*]

An enlightened yogi; one who lives in the state of unity-consciousness; one whose experience of the supreme Self is uninterrupted and whose identification with the ego has been dissolved.

SO'HAM [*so'ham*]

(*lit.*, I am That) *So'ham* is the mantra that expresses the natural vibration of the Self, which occurs spontaneously with each incoming and outgoing breath. By becoming aware of *So'ham*, a seeker experiences the identity between the individual self and the supreme Self.

SUDARSHANA CHAKRA [*sudarśanacakra*]

The discus carried by Lord Vishnu to protect his devotees and destroy evil.

TAPASYA [*tapasyā*]

(*lit.*, heat) 1) Austerities. 2) The fire of yoga; the heat generated by spiritual practices.

UPANISHADS [*upaniṣad*]

The inspired teachings, visions, and mystical experiences of the ancient sages of India. With immense variety of form and style, all of these scriptures (exceeding one hundred texts) give the same essential teaching: that the individual soul and God are one.

YAJNA MANDAP [*yajñamaṇḍapa*]

A pavilion in Gurudev Siddha Peeth Ashram where ancient fire ceremonies, *yajñas*, are performed.

YOGA [*yoga*]

(*lit.*, union) The spiritual practices and disciplines that lead a seeker to evenness of mind, to the severing of the union with pain, and through detachment, to skill in action. Ultimately, the path of yoga leads to the constant experience of the Self.

ABOUT
GURUMAYI CHIDVILASANANDA

*G*URUMAYI CHIDVILASANANDA is a spiritual teacher in the ancient yogic tradition of India. As the head of a lineage of meditation masters, she continues the time-honored role of sages in every tradition—helping seekers awaken to their own inner greatness and to the divinity inherent in the universe. Gurumayi follows in the footsteps of her spiritual master, Swami Muktananda, who brought the teachings and practices of Siddha Yoga meditation to the West in the 1970s, in what he called a "meditation revolution." In 1982, the last year of his life, he selected Gurumayi as his successor, and she was ordained as a swami, a monk in the Saraswati order. Swami Muktananda, known to his devotees as Baba, was himself the successor to Bhagawan Nityananda, a much-revered saint of modern India.

Gurumayi is often in residence at one of the spiritual retreat sites of Siddha Yoga meditation. The main retreat sites are in Ganeshpuri, India, and South Fallsburg, New York. Throughout the year, the wisdom and practices of the Siddha Yoga path are carried around the world by teaching monks and lay teachers.

GURUMAYI CHIDVILASANANDA

In this way, seekers of all nationalities are able to receive the grace of the Siddha Yoga lineage in their own homes, in their own languages, and in harmony with their own traditions.

Gurumayi's and Baba's work, administered by the SYDA Foundation, has inspired charitable and service initiatives. The PRASAD Project, an international humanitarian organization, assists children and families in need throughout the world with medical and dental care, education, and community relief programs. The Muktabodha Indological Research Institute is dedicated to the study, preservation, and dissemination of the ancient scriptural wisdom of India.

Gurumayi inspires seekers to cherish each moment of Self-revelation as a priceless gift from God. Along with teaching the spiritual practices of meditation, chanting, contemplation, and service, Gurumayi urges people to share their own goodness with others. She encourages everyone everywhere to translate into daily life their experiences of grace and their awareness of the great love residing in the human heart.

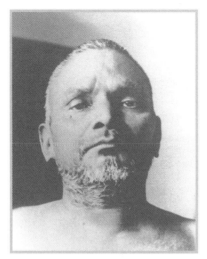

BHAGAWAN NITYANANDA

SWAMI MUKTANANDA

FURTHER READING

by
Gurumayi Chidvilasananda

COURAGE AND CONTENTMENT
Gurumayi illuminates the mysterious connections between courage and contentment, revealing the surprising origin of fear, the fundamental reason for loving yourself and others, the secret of transforming difficulties into blessings, and the way to create a life of abundance, service, and happiness.

ENTHUSIASM
"Be filled with enthusiasm and sing God's glory" is the theme of this collection of talks by Gurumayi. In these pages, she inspires us to let the radiance of enthusiasm shine through every action, every thought, every minute of our lives. This, Gurumayi says, is singing God's glory.

MY LORD LOVES A PURE HEART
The Yoga of Divine Virtues
Fearlessness, reverence, compassion, freedom from anger — Gurumayi describes how these magnificent virtues are an integral part of our true nature. The list of virtues introduced is based on chapter 16 of the *Bhagavad Gītā*.

THE YOGA OF DISCIPLINE
"From the standpoint of the spiritual path," Gurumayi says, "the term *discipline* is alive with the joyful expectancy of divine fulfillment." In this series of talks on practicing and cultivating discipline of the wandering senses, Gurumayi shows us how this practice brings great joy.

KINDLE MY HEART
The first of Gurumayi's books, this is an introduction to the classic themes of the spiritual journey. There are chapters on such subjects as meditation, mantra, control of the senses, the Guru, the disciple, and the state of a great being.

FURTHER READING

INNER TREASURES

"Every heart blazes with divine light," Gurumayi says. "Every heart trembles with divine love." In these inspiring talks, she offers us practical ways to cultivate the inner treasures: peace, joy, and love.

Poetry and Contemplation

SMILE, SMILE, SMILE!

Throughout the ages, great spiritual masters have offered their teachings in spontaneous outpourings of poetry. In these poems, Gurumayi demonstrates the mystical process of spiritual contemplation, offering the reader a deeper awareness of the perfection of the soul.

(Also available on audio cassette, read by the author.)

THE MAGIC OF THE HEART
Reflections on Divine Love

In these profound and tender reflections on divine love, Gurumayi makes it clear that the supreme Heart is a place we must get to know. It is here, she tells us, in the interior of the soul, that "the Lord reveals Himself every second of the day."

RESONATE WITH STILLNESS
Daily Contemplations by
Swami Muktananda, Swami Chidvilasananda

Every sentence of this exquisite collection of contemplations is an expression of wisdom and love from Baba Muktananda and Gurumayi Chidvilasananda. The selections are arranged around twelve themes of spiritual life, with a contemplation for each day of the year.

FURTHER READING

by
Swami Muktananda

PLAY OF CONSCIOUSNESS
In this intimate and powerful portrait, Baba Muktananda describes his own journey to Self-realization, revealing the process of transformation he experienced under the guidance of his Guru, Bhagawan Nityananda.

MUKTESHWARI
Baba Muktananda guides us through the stages of the spiritual path, inviting us to throw off our limitations and join him in the state of total freedom. These autobiographical verses are among Baba's earliest writings.

REFLECTIONS OF THE SELF
In aphoristic poetry, Baba reflects on the fundamental truths of spiritual life. A mixture of wisdom, prayer, and instruction, the book is infused with love — for the Self, for God, for the Guru.

FROM THE FINITE TO THE INFINITE
This compilation of questions and answers is drawn from Baba Muktananda's travels in the West. In it, Baba addresses all the issues a seeker might encounter on the spiritual path, from the earliest days until the culmination of the journey.

THE PERFECT RELATIONSHIP
In this classic work, Baba unravels the mystery of the sublime relationship between Guru and disciple. He draws upon his own experience and the Indian scriptures to demonstrate that inner freedom is attained by means of this profound relationship.

Library of Congress Cataloging-in-Publication Data

Chidvilasananda, Gurumayi.
[Ashes at my Guru's feet]
Pulsation of love / Gurumayi Chidvilasananda.
    p. cm.
"The poems in this volume were originally published in limited edition under
the title: Ashes at My Guru's Feet"—CIP data sheet.
Includes bibliographical references (p.)
  ISBN 0-911307-88-5 (pbk.)
  1. Chidvilasananda, Gurumayi. 2. Muktananda, Swami 1908- 3. Spiritual biography.
  4. Chidvilasananda, Gurumayi—Poetry. 5. Muktananda, Swami, 1908—Poetry. I. Title.
BL1283.792.C45 A325 2001
811'.54—DC21

00-010724

You may learn more about the teachings and practices
of Siddha Yoga meditation by contacting

SYDA FOUNDATION

PO BOX 600, 371 BRICKMAN RD

SOUTH FALLSBURG, NY 12779-0600, USA

TEL: 845-434-2000

or

GURUDEV SIDDHA PEETH

PO GANESHPURI, PIN 401 206

DISTRICT THANA, MAHARASHTRA, INDIA

Please visit our website at
www.siddhayoga.org

For further information on books in print by Swami Muktananda and
Swami Chidvilasananda, editions in translation, and audio
and video recordings, please contact

SIDDHA YOGA BOOKSTORE

PO BOX 600, 371 BRICKMAN RD

SOUTH FALLSBURG, NY 12779-0600, USA

TEL: 845-434-2000 EXT. 1700

Call toll-free from the United States and Canada: 888-422-3334
Fax toll-free from the United States and Canada: 888-422-3339